Letters to Myself
Volume 4
Abuse, Bullying, & Cults

By:
Award Winning &
#1 International Bestselling Author
Jen Taylor, LCSW

ELITE PUBLISHING
HOUSE
YOUR LEGACY. YOUR BOOK.

First Edition

Copyright 2024 © Jen Taylor, LCSW

All Rights Reserved

No part of this book may be reproduced or transmitted in any form or by any means, electronic or mechanical, including photocopying, recording or by an information storage and retrieval system – except by a reviewer who may quote brief passages in a review to be printed in a magazine, newspaper or on the Web – without permission in writing from the publisher.

Cover Graphics: Kathryn Denhof

ELITE PUBLISHING HOUSE
YOUR LEGACY. YOUR BOOK.

To my dear friend, Rhoda Finkelstein Galub,

who has witnessed me grow from a young child.

Thank you for your love, friendship, and support these

5 decades.

♥

United States:
If you or someone you know is experiencing a mental health, suicide crisis, or emotional distress, reach out 24/7 to the 988 Suicide and Crisis Lifeline (formerly known as the National Suicide Prevention Lifeline) by dialing or texting 988 or using chat services at suicidepreventionlifeline.org to connect to a trained crisis counselor.

Please see Appendix Suicide Resources for Worldwide Numbers

Bullying:
www.stopbullying.gov
https://www.crisistextline.org/topics/bullying/#what-is-bullying-1
www.stompoutbullying.org

Cyberbullying:
https://www.cybersmile.org/advice-help/category/who-to-call

Spiritual Abuse:
https://www.thehotline.org/resources/what-is-spiritual-abuse/

United States Resources:

National Sexual Assault Hotline: 800 656 HOPE
or www.rainn.org
(Rape, abuse, and incest national hotline)

National Domestic Violence Hotline: 800 787 7233
or www.thehotline.org

Planned Parenthood Hotline: 800 230 7526
or www.plannedparenthood.org

TABLE OF CONTENTS

FOREWORD 10
    Blair Hayse, International Speaker & Bestselling Author

INTRODUCTION 14

COLLECTION OF LETTERS 19

    Anonoymous

    Gene Yonish

    Anonoymous

    Marvin Ginsberg

    Anonoymous

    K.B.

    Singha

    Janet Sproule

    JS

    Jennifer Bynes

    Singha

    Anonoymous

    Victoria

    LM

JT

Lynsey Brown

Blair Hayse

MESSAGES OF HOPE 78

APPENDIX ON SUPPORT RESOURCES 80

APPENDIX ON SUICIDE RESOURCES 82

Includes Resources for Suicide Help & Assessment

CONDUCT A SUICIDE INQUIRY 95

DETERMINE RISK LEVEL 98

ABOUT THE AUTHOR 100

Foreword

Blair Hayse

International Speaker & Author

Jen Taylor has been in my world for several years now, weaving her way in and out of collaboration projects, speaking at events, and creating her own solo book series, which she allowed me the honor to publish. So, we are not strangers, but I can tell you that over the last few years, I have grown acutely aware that she was placed in my life for a reason beyond books or business, but as a kindred soul that I am sure I knew in another lifetime. Her empathy, love, compassion, and willingness to step into the gap to create a bridge of hope for those who need it in the most troubling of times, I have witnessed personally. I am unsure where my life would be without her because she has impacted my life so much. She is the definition of pure hope and love in a time when the world seems cruel and self-centered.

When Jen asked me to write the foreword for this particular book, I was honored and floored. How can little ole me be a writer of such a profound book's foreword? It is a book that I have watched her live, eat, and breathe life into for over a year now as she has intricately planned each detail of her volumes to ensure they have the most significant impact. As I sit here and pen my words into this foreword, I am moved to the brink of tears just by the subject of the book alone and the enormous amount of gratitude I have for her creating this series, but especially this particular volume.

Tucked far in my childhood past, I was part of a cult that my parents chose to join. A cult that tore apart my life as I knew it and cast upon me a curse that I am still dealing with many decades later. When one thinks of a cult, one thinks of crazy leaders asking their people to do ridiculous things, but honestly, cults can be tucked in the neatest packages, and you may never see the truth of them being a cult until you leave…or maybe never. Once you have been in a cult, gotten out, and received help to heal - you often see cults in the most ordinary places, right in plain sight, and tons of people are entrapped in their grips without even realizing it. Most of the time, if you feel like there is a "clique" mentality - that is the first red flag that maybe it is more of a cult than a community. Suppose individualism is overpowered by an acceptance of you *only* if you hold the same beliefs, standards, or choices as those in the clique or by the leader. In that case, you should carefully evaluate the community in which you are choosing. However, that is another topic for another day.

The lack of education and resources available for those leaving cults is sad, considering the modern times in which we live. The help and resources are scarce - leaving one vulnerable to returning to the familiar paths of the cult in which they wanted to leave or another cult to replace the one left. The cycle of being drawn to abusive relationships is a stigma the cult places on you, and you find yourself continually putting yourself in those unhealthy relationships over and over. Cults can cause one to have low self-worth, struggle with identity, and misplaced shame or guilt, to name a few of the long-term trauma effects. You have to figure out your own beliefs because you have become so entwined in what the cult has placed as values for you; that process alone can take a lifetime.

Due to my cult upbringing (which I did leave at eighteen), I was drawn back to abusive relationships over and over because my own identity and self-worth were at an all-time low. I found myself in domestic violence situations that endangered me and those closest to me. I found myself in abusive relationships, toxic personal friendships, low boundaries, misplaced guilt, and a struggle to create any self-worth in myself. To the outside world, I think many found me to be confident, and my mother used to say I was "proud," but what they did not see was the many hours behind closed doors where I questioned everything about myself and the tears I shed feeling "not good enough" for just about anything or anyone. Due to that, I sought validation in the worst possible places, and it made me vulnerable to those who hurt me, abused me, and used me. That pattern is typical in cults and abusive relationships - they are often intertwined and interconnected. It is said that 1 in 5 adults demonstrate the trauma symptoms of religious trauma, and 1 in 3 have been in a domestic violence relationship.

The serious long-term effects of cults can be life-changing, and I am grateful for Jen bringing awareness to subjects that are close to my heart and life. These subjects can change the trajectory of who you are and the life path you take. She chooses to be the voice in an overly silent, look-the-other-way world. The contributing authors within the series and this book are being transparent about their own experiences, and their transparency and bravery need to be applauded because their voices can change so many lives not to make the same choices, identify the patterns, have hope to choose different, and many more long-lasting impacts. I hope each of you read this book and find a voice for yourself in those voices shared.

If you find yourself in a relationship or community where you are not encouraged to be yourself or feel that something is wrong, reach out for help outside the circle. Trust yourself and your instincts that tell you something is not right.

Choose you. Always, always, always, choose you.

Introduction

Trigger warning

Abuse is based on power and control. Please see the cycles of violence graphic and power & control wheel.

*Retrieved from: https://www.safehousenm.org/power-and-control

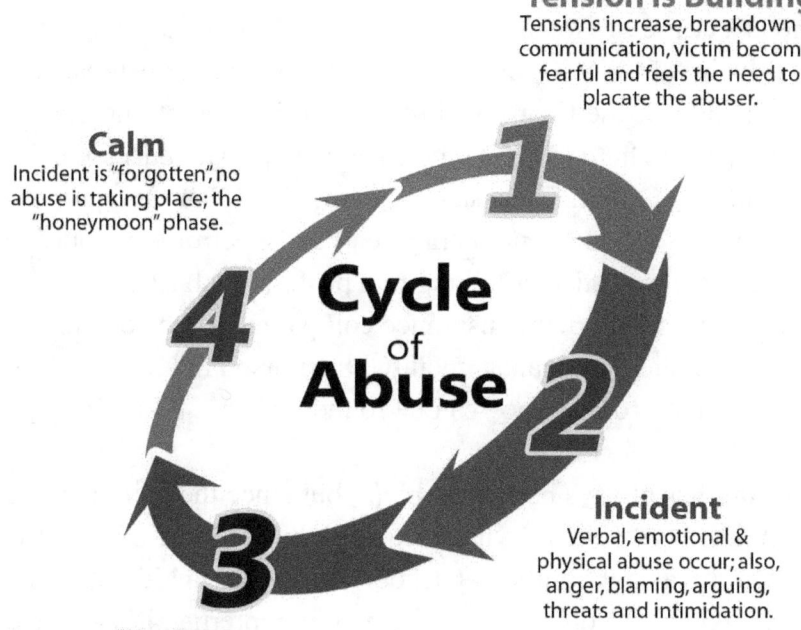

There are so many types and levels of abuse. Until recently, it was thought that physical abuse was the only actual type of severe abuse. In some cultures, abuse is accepted in a marriage or within family dynamics. Abuse includes physical, emotional, verbal, sexual, financial, and isolation. In the U.S., domestic violence (DV) came into public awareness in the 1970s. In NYC, Donna Ferrato partnered with some of the city's public health campaigns to bring awareness to domestic violence. Today in NYC, if you call 911 for a domestic dispute, a social worker will accompany the cops. While strides have been made in this field, we have a long way to go. In some marriages, it is considered acceptable for a partner to demand and expect sex from the other without consent. That, in fact, is rape. Unbeknownst to many, rape is a crime of violence. It is expressed through a sexual act, but it is, in fact, a **VIOLENT** crime. In many relationships, one person controls the finances; this is fine if it's something that is agreed upon. There is often emotional and verbal abuse, which is difficult to pinpoint. Some say, "It's how I talk" or "It's part of my culture." If you are not being treated respectfully in your relationship, please consider talking to a professional. Lifestance Health works with many insurance companies and offers talk therapy, medication management with a nurse practitioner or psychiatrist, and groups. They can be found at: https://lifestance.com/

Bullying has always been a problem, but since the entrance of social media, cyberbullying has escalated this issue. A friend mentioned, "I was only bullied at school when I was a kid. When I got home, I knew it would stop. Now, with the internet, it's 24/7." Sadly, cyberbullying has resulted in many suicides. If you are suicidal or know someone who needs support, please call 988 in The United States of America or go to the closest emergency room. Please see Volume 1 of Letters to Myself as a support with resources as well regarding this matter: https://www.amazon.com/dp/B0CLT6TXW1

Religious cults still exist today.

A cult is an organized group whose purpose is to dominate cult members through psychological manipulation and pressure strategies.1 Cults are usually headed by a powerful leader who isolates members from the rest of society. Some individuals who join cults remain lifelong members.

I remember the famous "Kool-Aid" cult from the Jonestown massacre in the 1970s. I know a few people who were born into religious cults. Our publisher, Blair, shares her own story in this volume. It is essential to understand that abuse and control are inherent in cult life. They set the stage for someone to become accustomed to this type of lifestyle. Abuse can come to feel comfortable because it is familiar. Familiarity does not mean it is healthy. If we are raised in abusive surroundings, we may look for or be drawn to abusive relationships as it is a dynamic that is familiar to us.

Know that healing is possible. It can be a long, challenging road. I have done many years of therapy and spiritual work, and I continue to work on myself.

A few of my excellent teachers, astrologers, intuitives, & coaches:

ELIZABETH MYERS:
Spiritual teacher, intuitive reader, dream interpreter.
mistletoex17@gmail.com

DINESH SINGH
Dineshkalyan67@gmail.com
Palm reader, numerologist, spiritual counselor & healer, ayurvedic consultant

DEMITRA VASSILIADIS:
Spiritual astrologer
Heaventoearthastrology.com

ELANA KILKENNY:
Intuitive counselor, sacred space design

Info@elanakilkenny.com

CANDICE PARISI:
Psychic medium
travelingintuitive.com

MOLLY MCCORD
Intuitive astrologer
www.MollyMcCord.online

TISCH AITKEN
Spiritual astrologer & writer
astroseek@aol.com

Also, I extend my heartfelt thanks to Elite Publishing and Blair Hayse, who helped me fulfill my lifelong dream of being an international bestselling author, and Kathryn Denhof, our talented graphic artist. Gratitude to the authors of this volume, both anonymous and named, without whom there would be no book.

Collection Of Letters

A STORY THAT NEEDS TO BE HEARD

This story is the truth from my perspective. I have changed the names of the characters. I am sure it is not the only story of its kind. I pray it does not seem familiar to you.

Dear Self,

The laundry is stacked to the ceiling today. I am waiting between loads. It is giving me time to think about things I need to clear out of my head. You, the me of the past, are coming to the end of another Summer. You are facing a difficult choice. Do you withdraw Samuel from school? How can you manage that as a single mom caring for two elder grandparents, working forty hours, and trying to finish school yourself? Trust me, you don't. Also, trust me, it is the best choice you will ever make. Take him out of school.

Samuel went into fifth grade as an average student. He was in a large class. The teacher, Ms. Mean Bitch targeted him and two other boys, Harold and Timothy, on the first day. Their school year would become days of torment. All three boys had things in common. They were all boys. They all came from single-parent homes. They were all below the poverty line. They all appeared to have no advocacy.

The first time you watched Samuel cry on Sunday morning because he did not want to go to school on Monday was heartbreaking. That first Sunday would begin a war that would be fought the whole school year. Spoiler alert: we lost this one badly. He would panic every day, trying not to forget anything at home. If he forgot a pencil, he was punished. The punishment was to stand in front of the class with a borrowed pencil and do his work standing up. He was denied recess for six weeks straight for minor infractions. The teacher meetings began. It was apparent that you - his mother - were a coddler who knew nothing of what needed to be done. You did not handle that well. Thankfully, you did not grab her by her hair and slam her head on the desk.

Next, we went to Mr. Principle. He played solitaire on his computer in front of you. That lets you know how little he felt about you or your issues. When he finally had time to address your concerns, all he said was that Ms. Mean Bitch was his best teacher and that your son was exaggerating things. That was infuriating. Meanwhile, every day was a torment for both Samuel and you. You would hate sending him to school.

The incidents gathered in number, and so did your desperation. He left his glasses at home one day. Not wanting for him to get in trouble, you brought them up to the school. They held his glasses for a week, then threatened to call child services if you did not fix the problem. You threatened to sue them if they did not return the glasses. The glasses were returned.

One day, Harold and Timothy visited the house for a Boy Scout project. That is when you realized it was not just Samuel who was having issues. You learned that Harold had marks on his arm from where Ms. Mean Bitch grabbed him. You talked to his dad. He did report it to Mr. Principle, but nothing was done about it. Timothy had similar stories as Samuel. His mom had cancer and did not have the strength to fight.

Samuel's torments got worse. The school even denied him having his rescue inhaler at the school. You have to call the State School Board of Nursing to get them to accept it. Next, you will call your School Board Representative to demand an investigation of Ms. Mean Bitch. Nothing is done. You will fight tooth and nail for your child right up until the last day of school. Nothing will be done.

We talk about bullying from other kids. Sometimes, that is condoned from the top down. Kids take their cues from the leaders of the school. They find the most vulnerable by watching the top tier.

Pull Samuel out of school. I know you do. Don't worry about it. He is brilliant. He will get his high school diploma on his own. He will become a wonderful man with a great career. He will even travel the world. You don't know it now, but it is the best choice you will ever make for him.

Harold will carry the fingernail scars on his arm for the rest of his life. He grows up to work with his dad in the industry. He marries a nice woman. All his kids are homeschooled, and he openly advocates against public education.

Timothy's mom will die of cancer. He did not pass the 6th grade. Facing another year in 5th grade, he will end his life on the last day of this summer. This will be what pushes you to make the choice to withdraw Samuel from school.

Mr. Principle and Ms. Mean Bitch will have some small justice served them when they are both arrested for embezzling school funds.

We have a hard road to tread now. As Christians, it is part of our spiritual path to embrace forgiveness. I am telling you, from my past, that 24 years later, I would still push those two underwater if I saw them drowning. I have no forgiveness in my heart for them. I guess if I could tell you to do anything different, I would say go ahead and grab that bitch by the hair and slam her head on the desk like you wanted to. It will be worth going to jail for. I know you don't, but it would be therapeutic if you did.

Bullying does not start with children. It starts with adults. It starts with what children see and learn from the adults around them. What is acceptable behavior? It is what we show them. If there is a bullying problem in school, one should ask what the adults are doing that says it is ok.

Now, I tell people who are facing a similar case not to waste time. Just homeschool your kids. Staying for the good fight is a long waste of time.

Oh, look, it's time to put on another load of clothes. You don't have to forgive Ms. Mean Bitch and Mr. Principle. You do have to forgive yourself. You did the best you could without going to jail.

Sincerely,

You

-Anonymous

Different Than My Dad

Emotional abuse,
There ain't no excuse.
Transferred rage,
As if he were trapped in a cage.
Seething inside,
Against me and his bride.
Caustic words,
They were loudly heard.
Sense of reasoning blurred.
Mood so quickly changed,
Acting like someone deranged.
My dad had issues,
Experienced, often much blued.
Holocaust issues experienced by many Jews.
What can I learn,
To not be the same?
Feelings churn,
Feelings to tame.
Stay cool, collected, and calm.
Words mean,
And caustic.
Stop yelling like an immature teen.
Words sick.
I can be different and be an emotional balm.

-Gene F Yonish

Abuse:
Something easy to fall for; I fell.

From an outside perspective, you can see those who have been abused and those who are traumatized, but you never think it'll be you in the 80%.

In June of 2022, I met this boy. We were getting to know each other and I noticed that I started to really like him. We met a week later in downtown Manhattan. I was with him and a few of my friends. Minutes after we met, he had already made a move. He took my hand into his. I found that weird because we haven't even had a real conversation yet. He didn't ask what I liked to do or what I looked for in a relationship. He just took my hand. Obviously, holding my hand was not sexual, but this was the start of him playing the part of a sweet, innocent boy that he definitely wasn't. If that wasn't the start of it, him telling me everything I have ever wanted to hear from a guy was. Manipulation. He was using his way of words to coax me into his trap. He wanted to say everything that convinced me he loved me even when he didn't. All he wanted was to get what he wanted. He didn't want to love a sweet girl who had never had a boyfriend before, who had never felt love from a guy who just wanted teenage love.

That same day, he slept at my house for two weeks straight—zero contact with his mother. It was just him taking advantage of the time he had with me. When we got to my home (me, him, and my friends), the first thing he wanted to do was cuddle up close to me. It felt good to think someone had an emotional connection with me. It felt good to see he felt safe with me and wanted to be close to me. I was a girl who liked a guy, and he made me feel good about myself, so I thought it was normal even though it was only in the first few hours of getting to know each other. Later that night, as my friends were falling asleep, he started to initiate wanting to kiss me, and I agreed to it. I got uncomfortable with the fact that my friends were in the same room sleeping while I was making out with a boy I had just met. I'm not sure how I was okay sleeping next to a boy I knew nothing about besides what he told me when meeting him that same day. He started to initiate going further than making out, and I told him it was awkward and uncomfortable, given I just met him and my friends were over. He was nice about it, and I felt at ease knowing he wouldn't push me to do anything I didn't want to do until he did.

We get to July, and this is where the abuse starts. I notice he's more distant, aggressive, rude, and selfish. It begins with him disappearing from my sight for a day without any realistic explanation. At least not one that was believable. He said he was going to a guy's house who does investments so that he can make money for himself, his family, and me. He turned his location off, and he disappeared for 7 hours. I didn't hear from him until late at night when he said he would meet me at my house. I told him I was confused about why he would go off somewhere and have zero communication with me; I was worried and scared. I told him it wasn't fair to have plans with me that day and disappear, especially under my responsibility. I told him that he clearly wasn't respecting me because he knew how bad my anxiety was, and the least he could do was tell me he was okay after 30 missed calls throughout the 7 hours he was gone. He began to say to me I was crazy, controlling, annoying, and clingy. All because I was worried about a boy who I liked. I vividly remember sitting on my steps. I didn't feel safe sitting alone with him as he already had a tone and was aggressive with his voice and hand gestures. I asked my friend to sit with us just in case he snapped. Even though my friend was there, he raised his voice and called me "dramatic" and "too much." I said he was welcome to go home if he was going to keep calling me names and continue to invalidate me. He brainwashed me into thinking that I had gotten the wrong time for when he would be back. He told me I was calling him like a crazy person. He told me he deserved freedom when all I gave him was that. I just wanted a reassuring answer to know he was okay. Later that night, he initiates a sexual act. Looking back at it now, I see that this seems to be how he handled arguments or disagreements most of the time. Manipulation. Over the span of July, he kept invalidating me. He called me crazy far too many times. He told me I was being dramatic. Later that month, we were making out, and I was on top of him, getting to a more intimate point. While we were doing sexual things, he would say, "I love you." That was the only time he would say it. I could say for myself that that was highly manipulative and wrong. I didn't say it back because it was so fast and only a few weeks into knowing him. It felt wrong, and I didn't know if I loved him yet.

One night, I said I wasn't okay with something he did. Simply just communicating with him as people should in relationships. He had a massive freak out, saying that he wanted to go home and that I always made everything an issue. No, he kept crossing boundaries and disrespecting me. He started yelling at me in front of my friend who was there. I told him to stop yelling at me. He gave me the silent treatment for 30 minutes, so I asked him if we could talk in the hallway. We speak in the hallway, and I tell him how I feel. He continued to yell and say that I made a fool out of him in front of my friend. I did not make a fool out of him; I stuck up for myself because I don't allow those who claim they love me to yell at me. He once again calls me dramatic in the hallway. Nothing new. The next day me, him, and my friend went to a makeup store. My friend brings up a conversation we had regarding him. I asked if we could stop talking about it because it was a conversation between me and my friend for a reason. Not me, him, and my friend.

There are texts showing on my phone of our conversation because I forgot exactly what we talked about regarding him, so he grabs my arm with a firm grip, leaving a mark saying, "Let me see," in an aggressive tone. I tell him to let go of me and to never touch me like that again, or we're breaking up. He said, "I did not grab you. I held your arm in my hand." I told him he left a red mark, which he did. He tells me what I saw and makes me second guess myself even though I saw a red mark as soon as he let go of me. "There was no red mark; stop lying to me and making your friend believe that I hurt you." She did see that he hurt me. She saw the whole thing. There was no going back from him grabbing me in that store. He doesn't apologize; he just grabs my waist and pulls me in for a hug. I expressed that I did not want a hug, and he said, "Okay, you don't have to be like that. Nothing bad happened. You're exaggerating." My friend and I step aside, and she asks if I'm okay. I say I'm fine, and she says, "I'm really sorry that I need to tell you this, but that was physically abusive of him." I immediately stepped my foot down and totally disagreed with the fact that it was abuse. I was even upset that she would say that. We get to the cashier, and he acts like everything is normal. Being the sweetest boy can be to the cashier, making it seem like we're a perfectly happy couple even after what just happened.

Towards the middle of the month, two bigger events happened in our relationship. The first one was when my friend was over. He randomly asked me to go to the bathroom because he had to use it. As I am someone who goes to the bathroom with my best friends, I would also go with my boyfriend, having no sexual intentions and just using the bathroom together. I noticed that he was sexually aroused. I said, "I don't want to do anything like that right now. I'm not in the mood, but my friend is here." His response was manipulative, selfish, and unacceptable. "I'm already hard, and if you don't give me what I need, it'll hurt. Please?"

I felt bad. I felt pressured. And so, I did. I did give him what he "needed." I felt gross after. I wasn't into it. I didn't want to give him a hand job, as I expressed. I was scared that he would be mad at me if I didn't. He was already angry when I leaned towards no, so I did it. A few weeks later, I went to my friends and told them what happened in the bathroom. I said it was wrong of me even to say yes. I expressed that I felt terrible and shouldn't have done that. The last thing they did was blame me. They made me aware that he pressured me into something I didn't have to do. I dismissed it. I said it was okay because I thought it was.

I always excused him. In the next two weeks, a significant event happened in my life. He raped me. By the boy, I thought, loved me. By the boy who told me, I was beautiful and deserved the world. By the boy who told me, he would never hurt me. I told him I wanted to stop because I didn't feel well, and he said he was almost there. I told him it hurt, and he said he was sorry, but he kept going. I said stop, but he just kept going. No matter what I said, he kept going. I didn't talk about it for a year and a half. I knew it was wrong, and I knew I said no, but I didn't want to label it. I told my therapist last summer, and she told me that what happened; was rape. I was in shock. I was disgusted. I didn't know what to do or how to tell my parents.

I just kept it in until I was ready. I was never ready. I asked my therapist to go into more depth on our session with my mom so that I didn't have to. A month ago, I had my first physical reaction to my rape. I had a panic attack triggered by an educational episode on sexual abuse. I had to turn it off. I had to wake up my mom. My dad had to go get her because I couldn't move. I couldn't breathe. I remember texting two of my friends, saying that I felt like I was shutting down and that they were trying to keep me as grounded as possible until my mom got to the living room. At that moment, I didn't know what was going to happen. I felt lost.

I thought that everything this boy was telling me was real. I thought he loved me. I thought he wanted to be with me. I thought he loved me for me, not my body. I was wrong. I was manipulated. He took advantage of my bubbly and kind personality. I tried to get out of it three times. The average amount of times women try to get out of abusive relationships is seven. Sometimes it's too late. I am more than thankful for my friends. They knew what I was going through wasn't normal. It wasn't okay. They were scared for me. They are part of the reason I got out of it. Two of my best friends stuck by me the whole time. From the first page of this chapter to the last. I never thought I would get out. I thought I would be stuck forever with the constant emotional abuse, the grabbing, and the rape. I didn't know if I could do it. But I did. I got through it, and I got out of it.

You're not alone if you're reading this and have been through something similar. I am right here. I am someone who went through this, and I got out of it. As hard as it may be, I believe you can too. Whatever happens, no matter how scared you are, turn to a friend, a parent, a sibling, or a cousin. Whoever you're comfortable with, ask them for help or support. You're not alone in this. It does get better; you heal, grow, and evolve, and find a boy who will show you what love really is. The love you've never felt before. The love you never thought you would feel. You gain self-love and confidence. You start a new chapter of your life. You grow stronger and stronger by the day. YOU. You are strong and capable. You're loved. You have people standing with you.

-Anonymous

Dear_____,

Love yourself.

You are important. You are amazing. You have so much to give.

Who are the bullies in your life?

Who do they remind you of in childhood?

That's what created the programming. As a result, everyone is a bully.

Your family bullies are now the human family. As we get older, our family becomes larger.

The bully has become your voice in your head in a continuous loop.

Is that the program you want? Is that your mantra you want?

You can change it.

You can change your whole world by letting it go.

Your world is in your head, your perception.

Let's look at it differently.

Let the thoughts go.

Let them go. Release them. Don't judge them or evaluate them.

They are not you.

Sing them. Dance to them. Let them go. Create a melody.

It's your morning dance.

The thoughts- will vanish. You will feel better and better. You will feel joy. Try it

What's to lose?

You can love yourself.

Part two:

What do you want to do in your life?

What's your vision?

What kind of a world would you like to see?

What kind of a life would you like to have?

Start here.

If you need help, contact me.

Mordechai Baruch Ginsberg

Glowbility.com.

-Marvin Ginsberg

Well, I don't know where to start. Right now, I'm 58 years old, play music for a living, and am pretty well adjusted - as well as I can be at this stage in this environment. I have built a successful music business for 17 years and have a 20-year-old trans son. I'm divorced, and this is how it goes. I was asked to write about my childhood experiences and how it led to where I am today for these stories. I'm not very comfortable writing, so I will do my best to make it as clear as possible. With that being said, let's begin:

I'll start with my childhood. I am the firstborn of Italian immigrants in the US. My mother came here in 1959, and my father was the firstborn of his family. Both are from Sicily - meaning they are very "old-school." As a result, I grew up with certain superstitions. All this shaped my childhood in ways that most Americans can't understand. With that comes all the immigrant guilt, problems, and superstitions that come along with coming from another country where your family lives half in the Old World and half in America. I was the firstborn after my mother lost a child in Saudi Arabia (where she and my father lived after their marriage.) In my experience, the first male child is usually very loved and cherished, almost spoiled. I'm not spoiled, but I definitely know I was loved at home.

My early childhood had nothing but good memories. I will say, though, that my father, who was a high school teacher by trade and coming from an immigrant family, was kind of a "tiger" parent. I was taught to read early using flashcards for words and then moved on to reading books. I used
flashcards for math problems, et cetera. By the time I entered kindergarten, I was already reading and doing simple math, and I

35

found it interesting. That's where the problems started. I would say I was advanced for my age. I went through the typical path of a New York City public school system: kindergarten, first grade, and second grade. At that age, kids are pretty much all the same. Third grade was okay, but the problems started happening in the fourth grade. At that point, I got tested. Being so-called "gifted," I was put into a special advanced class with the other gifted students in my public elementary school. That is where I started getting bullied, and it went on for years. I was highly advanced but also a very physically small child and socially awkward. I found most of my classmates to be crude; that would be the word. Some of them were extremely intelligent, and some of them became lifetime best friends. The bullying and abuse started very gradually.

All young kids tease and taunt each other and play around, but after some time in the fourth grade, it really started to be aimed at me specifically. During lunch hours and play times after lunch, a group of kids gave me cruel nicknames. They would circle me and taunt me to no end. They would take some of my belongings, such as my bag or jacket, and play "keep away." That happened daily so that lunchtime was not spent playing ball but spent taunting me, and as a 10-year-old boy in fourth grade, it started to get to me. I would tell my parents, and my father, being an old-school Brooklyn guy, would tell me to "suck it up," that kids are just bad and whatever else he would apparently say, but it wasn't like empathy. That would be a recurring theme in my life, especially with my father. He told me that real men "suck it up," and they don't get affected or cry about things done by outside forces. He would say that typical parent thing, "Don't cry, or I'll give you something to cry about." My mother, on the other hand, loved me unconditionally.

This bullying went on from fourth grade through sixth grade, a solid two years. At one point during lunch, I was actually beaten up by a bunch of girls, which, as an 11-year-old boy, is not really good for your ego or mental health. All this would lead me to being socially awkward, reading constantly, and not having many friends. The friends that I did have were very loyal and good for my mental health. In fact, my childhood friend was not in my gifted class. He was a cool local kid, and I would like to thank him for helping me through these challenging times.

During this time, I retreated into books. I was a voracious reader. I read books in school when everyone else was paying attention to what was going on in class. I brought books with me everywhere I went, mostly science-fiction fantasy, even nonfiction history, you name it. That turned out to be a problem as I wasn't paying attention in class, and I would use the books to escape. There were entire worlds in those books, worlds where young kids had adventures. I have a vivid memory of getting a nasty cold and having to stay home from school for a few days. At age 10, over three days, I read the entire Lord of the Rings trilogy. Over the next few years, I reread that trilogy multiple times. This obsession with reading engulfed every part of my life. If the family went away to visit another family or for vacation, I would bring books with me. It got so out of hand that my mother would kick me out of the house so I could have some outdoor playtime with other children. I got around this by hiding books outside of my home so I could go down the block to the park and read. I would say those books saved my life and my psyche at a young age. Books and my library card were the keys that opened the doors of the world for me. When I read, nobody harassed me or bothered me. Lit fully engaged my brain in ways nothing else did.

The New York City School system is set up where you go to school K through 6, sixth through eighth grade, and then high school. Sixth through eighth is called junior high, and I entered junior high school with many of these same kids. The abuse and bullying continued. It was not as relentless as it had been before, but due to the type of school it was and because we changed classes, it was not as severe. What did go on at this time was my extremely high anxiety about being the perfect student. That was due to my father's "tiger' parenting style. What I mean by this is from the young age of, let's say, seven all the way through to age fifteen, I was told that they would look at my school record to go to college. If I did not have good grades, I would starve and be in danger of not surviving. That was an everyday occurrence with my father. During these years, I excelled most of the time and even took college classes and accelerated learning on the weekends and after school. At this point, I was 13 years old, and I developed an ulcer due to all the stress that my father put me through to achieve over and over again to get perfect grades. Even my loving mother was in on the action. If I showed up with a 95 on a test, her response would be, why did you not get 100%? I was very stressed out as a 13-year-old. One story I can share with you is that, at one point, I took a math test and received an 80 on it, and I refused to go home because I could not show my parents that grade. I was worried about the punishment that I would receive, such as tongue lashing. No way does this mean I had bad parents. Looking back, I realize they were doing what they thought was best for me. Now, as an adult, I realize I am slightly on the spectrum and have ADHD and anxiety. Even though my father was educated, he did not have the knowledge of how to deal with me. Before his death, my father told me how abused he was by his family after his father's death when he was about 10.

He had no good role models and always did his best to be the father he thought I needed. A lot of the time, it seemed to be parental bullying. All the other kids got driven to Boy Scouts meetings and soccer games, but my father would make me walk. He forced me to do a lot of things. I realize now he was teaching me to be an adult and a good man. When I went to college, even though we had the means, he consistently tried to make me go broke. He was not generous in that way because he did very well in life, having been motivated by not having anything. My father thought that same approach would make me very successful, more successful than he was. His American dream was that each generation would do better than the previous one. He convinced me at age ten that I would become a doctor or a chiropractor. As the story progresses, we will see how I became a larger disappointment.

As I stated earlier, my mother loved me with all her heart, but coming from a completely different culture, my mother had certain ideas and behaviors that I did not understand. For her, the clothing you wore, how you looked, and how clean your house was were measures of one's status. Only as an adult did I realize that my mother loved showing off vis a vis on my accomplishments. By that, I mean she would always tell everyone how advanced I was in school, how good my grades were, etc. That is where it gets interesting. My father was a depression-era child who was the son of immigrants. He had a very rough upbringing. He was not exposed to a lot of things. He was very aware of this, so he decided to give my sister things he did not have access to as a child.

Besides playing soccer, taking us to off-Broadway plays, and traveling, one of those things was making sure that we had music lessons. You could say these are things he did not have access to when he grew up and wanted for us. He forced me to have guitar lessons. He found a local music school, purchased a cheap acoustic guitar, and my weekly guitar lessons started. I was required to practice 30 minutes daily, the time kept by a baking timer. He would listen and make sure we practiced 30 minutes daily, six days a week. He said he wouldn't pay for lessons if I didn't put in the work. This went on for four years.

For the first two years, I did not enjoy it at all. For the next two, I did not hate it. At the end of the four years, when I was 12, I would listen to the radio and be fascinated by the guitar. At 11, my grandmother (Nonna) gave me an electric guitar for Christmas. It was inexpensive and cheap, but to me, it was the entire world. At this point, I realized the lessons I was going to were not teaching me anything further. I asked my father to find me a different teacher. He did. This teacher went on to run the entire music college years later. His name was Peter Rogine. He was very disciplined and started me on my journey. He got so busy that one of his students then gave me lessons. At this point, while attending junior high, guitar became an obsession.

I would come home every day before my parents got home from work and practice. My father, a teacher, introduced me to one of his colleague's sons, who was also obsessed with guitar. I would spend weekends at his house, and we would play guitar for over 12 hours a day. I became obsessed with the Beatles and played every song. I have a book called The Beatles Complete. I then moved on to 70s rock 'n roll. As the 80s emerged, I was fully immersed. I was still a nerdy, nerdy, dorky, awkward early teenager. At this point, I started growing my hair, which disappointed my entire family.

At 14, I tested into the top high school in New York City. In fact, it was probably the best high school in the entire United States at the time. I lived in Queens, and the school is on the Lower East Side of Manhattan. That is where my life started to change. I had to take a bus into Brooklyn and then the train for the final part of my trip. That was 1980. At that time, New York was still recovering from the 1970s; it was not as safe as it is today.

Going to school was a big eye-opener. I was meeting kids from all over New York City, all walks of life, and every nationality, and we were all bright and intelligent. At first, it was difficult, but I got used to it and even enjoyed it when it opened my eyes. The bullying stopped. All these kids were nerds and dorks in their schools. They were gifted and intelligent. I was treated with respect, and I felt at home. For the first two years, I was a good student. As time went on, my ego started to get crushed, and teenage rebellion kicked in. I no longer felt smart or special. That's how I dealt with all the bullying in my elementary school. I would tell myself I'm smarter than these kids; they're just dumb and ignorant. This strategy of dealing with my mental health did not work here. All these kids were much more intelligent and brighter than I was. That, combined with all the pressure my family put on me, initiated a significant change in my life. I found out that colleges only look at the last two years of your high school grades. I got extremely agitated, realizing my father and family stressed me for no reason. I was in a state of anxiety from the bullying from my classmates and the pressure from my family to succeed. At this point, I became somewhat of a delinquent. I was still bright and would go to classes when I liked the teachers. If I did not like the teacher, I would cut the class. My grades plummeted.

My home life became quite difficult. I grew my hair and threw myself into guitars and music. My mother, who loved telling her friends I was going to the best school in the country, was now embarrassed about me and how I looked. At the time, my music skills grew incrementally. Instead of doing homework, I would come home from school and practice guitar. Since I could not compete academically at this school, I used my music skills to set me apart. As I got better at my instrument, my self-confidence grew. I could perform, get applause, and be known as the "rock guitar guy." That followed me for the rest of my life.

I created a new persona. I fabricated a confident, outgoing persona to hide my insecurities and anxieties. During my 20s, I took it very far. I curated the way I looked with laser like precision. My hair, my clothing, and even my swagger. It was all to hide my insecurities until it became my actual identity. I went away to college for two years and lived in Buffalo, New York, but I could not stop thinking about making music my career. While at school, I gained weight. I became so self-conscious that I came back to New York and lost 35 pounds in two months. I wanted a music career, and at that time, how you looked mattered. I returned home to New York City, went to school part-time, and started joining bands. That has been my life since then. Now, at the age of 58, this has come back to haunt me. I was married, had a child, and got divorced, all the while playing music. Now, as I am aging, I have had to kill off this persona I created. I have had to come to terms with aging, my looks, my body, and my mind. For a while, this was quite difficult. I used my musicianship and my vocation as a shield to protect that little boy who was bullied for years. It made me feel special, but now I know I can be who I am. I cut off all my hair, and I do my best to stay slim, but I am chubby and have come to peace knowing I'm that nerdy, dorky person on the spectrum. It took me a long time to feel comfortable being that guy. I don't have to be special. I just have to be a good father to my child and a good person.

-Anonymous

I remember in second grade when my father and brother got into a fight, and my father threatened to "rip his fucking head off." I don't remember the reason, but that day, when I was seven and my brother was nine, their relationship deteriorated. Around this time, my dad started drinking again.

In fifth grade, I remember crying to my friend after my dad grabbed my wrist and hurt me. It wasn't intentional; it was never intentional. In seventh grade, I told my dad he had a problem, that he was an alcoholic. He denied it.

By the time I was in eighth grade, my brother had become "cool." Once a slightly chubby nerd, he had developed abs and started smoking weed. My father took pride in this; he always cared about what people thought of him and believed their opinions of us, his kids, mattered. At family reunions, he would brag to my cousins about my brother's weed use, claiming it made him "cool" and "popular." In hindsight, this was likely a way of validating his own addiction.

In ninth grade, I noticed my brother was smoking every night. I told my mom. Nothing was done.

In November of 11th grade, my brother started dabbling in hard drugs. On Christmas Day, he tried coke, claiming it was "festive" because it was the "snowy drug." He came downstairs, and it was apparent he was on some type of substance. It was then my dad realized he needed to stop drinking; that by drinking every night and occasionally smoking weed with my brother, he had been reinforcing his behavior.

My dad quitting alcohol was terrifying. Compared to when I was younger, his anger issues had gotten significantly better, and I wasn't sure if this was because he started drinking again or because he got a better therapist. Though it was selfish, I often wished he wouldn't quit drinking due to a fear of him reverting back to his old self. During this time, my parents finally got my brother some help, though it didn't work.

In May of 11th grade, my parents told me about the intervention they were planning for my brother. They had caught him ordering hard drugs to the house and realized if doing drugs was worth this risk, his problem was a lot worse than they thought. The following month, we had the intervention. During that intervention was the first time I saw my brother cry.

As I'm writing this, I'm going into 12th grade. I wish I could say these events didn't affect me, but I'd be lying. I fear addiction more than anything else, whether it's me getting addicted or the people I care about. In some way, that fear is a good thing. I'll never be peer-pressured into vaping. In other ways, it's bad and can lead me to be controlling about the habits of people I care about.

-K.B.

I would like to introduce myself. My name is Singha. I hope my story brings strength to people who have been abused and bullied. I lived in an ashram in India from the age of 16 to 23. It was an amazing place to be. I have learned everything there, such as caring and being kind to others…but when I came into the real world, I had to face many kinds of issues like bullying. I know it's really hard for a teenage girl or boy to face things like this; many of them are not capable of handling it emotionally, and it has a bad effect on them. Seeing the society, they might carry bitterness within themselves for people and society.

I was a yoga practitioner and a long-time meditator, so events such as bullying or abuse did not affect me, but yes, I could see everything that had been thrown at me. I came to realize that it's human behavior. I'm not talking about everyone, but yes, in this material and competitive world, humans have forgotten to be kind and sensitive…bullying and abuse have become a part of human behavior.

I want to share my experience. I hope it helps those who are struggling as victims. When, as humans, we become egoless and less angry, then we are able to become less bothered about things that are done by people who don't have sympathy for human life and human feelings. Such people need to be consulted because I feel they are the victims…victims of being rude and emotionless humans. They are becoming heartless, and that's not good for our society and humanity. I think we need to take care of them… rather than taking care of those who are getting abused and bullied by them …I know sometimes it's really hard for kids who are in their teens. Still, they must realize that hate is not the answer to hate…we can win hate with love. If we spit on the sky, it lands on our faces…so beautiful, gentle, don't become revengeful…just smile and walk away…yes, if it happens at the physical level, then please complain to the responsible authority.

Thank you so much.

-Singha

I have experienced bullying throughout my life, from primary school to high school, and then when working with various organizations. It has affected my mental health significantly, as well as my self-esteem. In school, they made fun of what I said, what I did, how I looked, and what my father did for a living. It was so bad at one point that my usually good grades had slipped dramatically. When my mother attended a parent-teacher night, the teacher told her I needed to "toughen up." The culprit was never punished, only the person receiving the abuse.

As an adult, I experienced many forms of bullying at work: struggling to make friends, being made fun of for who I am and what I do (subtly, of course), humiliated in front of others for mistakes I made or things I forgot to do. It led to my working extended hours to do my work under less pressure and avoid people criticizing me. I also felt immense pressure to complete my work daily and leave nothing to the next day. I experienced extreme anxiety, panic attacks, and depressive episodes. I didn't sleep well or at all as I was constantly reviewing what I had done that day to confirm that I missed nothing. I had several short periods of sick leave due to my mental health, and at the time, there was no recourse for me.

Over time, I learned to understand some of the reasons that the bullying occurred, how to cope with it, when to report it, and when to remove myself from toxic situations and people.

I am passionate about helping others who are bullied through my lived experience and have zero tolerance for bullying of any kind.

- Janet Sproule

Bullying seemed to follow me in intermittent cycles of my life. The first was through a man I would never consider to be a father to me. My parents separated when I was young. As a way to get back at my mother, the man who, unfortunately, is my father would call me just to verbally abuse me whenever he was in the mood to do so. Or call child services to make my mother's life a living hell, ignoring the fact that it made me anxious, nervous, and scared to be taken away from my mother, my home, and my haven.

Or a school bully who never seemed to stop feeling threatened by me. Numerous reasons accumulated in her relentless bullying of how we were raised. My mother spoiled me every chance she could when I did well in school, and I did so being a scholarship kid. That girl's mother would not do the same to her. The fact that I skipped a grade and was and still am close and open with my mother were all reasons the girl would not let up. Even after she tried getting 30 girls to jump my mother and I while on a school trip to the Museum of Natural History and managed to manipulate the principal from our school to side with her and push for me to leave the school. Even when I was in another school, she still managed to follow me there and wait for me. Luckily for me, we never crossed paths during that time.

As for us being adults now, with her one-sided attempts to bully me and make herself feel better, I see her occasionally as we live next to each other's apartment buildings. I see her as someone who peaked in high school and didn't bother studying. She couldn't even finish her primary education. Nor is she someone anyone in our old school would even consider a friend now, and who doesn't even have a high school diploma. She has no friends or partners and scurries away, terrified whenever we cross paths.

Sometimes, time can be the cruelest fate for those who never thought they would fall.

Lastly, my cousin, who wanted to be the center of attention, made comments about me going to jail or saying I was fat or that I looked like a raccoon from spending nights reading. Or she enjoys giving backhanded compliments that bite more than praise. As a child, I said nothing and would cry about it. The fact of telling people she would bully me only flitted about once through my mind, and I followed through. Still, most family members didn't realize it was a recurring experience, so it discouraged me, and I stayed quiet, especially if I was called a rat. And so the bullying continued until I simply was able to ignore it until I was an adult when she tried to bully me online; I finally put my foot down and called her out. As much as I love her and feel the pull of familial loyalty towards her, I refuse to be taken advantage of and be put down by someone who feels insecure and on the wrong footing with themselves. Though she is no longer close to me, it felt good to speak my peace.

As I have gotten older, I noticed that bullies will hurt you in their effort to hurt the one they originally intended to chip away at. The best way to leave that person is in peaceful silence; your accomplishments will make them suffer. Others will do so because they've reached their peak in life and live in reminisce. It's best to give them all the rope they need to hang themselves proverbially. At the same time, some will do so to hide their insecurities and flaws and eventually be confronted. Those will have to face the mirror that they can no longer keep verbally and emotionally using a silent person as their punching bag just because said person is family. Each has one thing in common: none achieved the satisfaction in me conforming to their whims.

To those who have been bullied and have moved on or are slowly moving on - have you realized your strength and courage in staying kind to others and not following the vicious cycle?

– JS

When you grow up in a home that displays abuse, as much as you want to be greater than what you witnessed, you sometimes fall into the pattern without realizing it. I was 19 when I met Rick. He was older and seemed so mature, and I was immediately enamored. I should have questioned why a man in his 20s wanted a young single mom, but hindsight is 20/20. Things were pretty exciting in the beginning. I didn't realize as time went on how he was isolating me from my friends and family; I didn't think anything of it. When my cousin, who was there for me more than anyone, tried to warn me and made me choose between him and her, or when I got into a physical altercation with my mother because of him. It didn't even dawn on me the first time he choked me in the train station; why, I don't remember, or when he choked me in the break room at work because he got me a job where he worked and was my supervisor.

I did not allow it to sink in that I was in an abusive relationship until I found out I was pregnant on Thanksgiving. My six-year-old saw her mom get her head slammed into a concrete wall. I had a severe concussion and still blamed myself. I knew I deserved better, but I didn't know how. I knew that I could not be connected to this man forever, so I terminated my pregnancy, moved back in with my mom, and stopped communicating with him four months later. He did apologize. He asked me not to get rid of the baby. His family begged. But seeing my daughter watching me get hit took me to a memory of watching my mother being choked and pushed into a closet while holding my newborn baby sister. I was also 6. It took a long time to heal from that, and I still blame myself for not being smarter or seeing the signs. They say you don't know when you are in it how deep the trauma runs. Luckily, my daughter is better and wiser and has never put herself in that situation, so I am grateful for that.

-Jennifer Bynes

I would like to introduce myself. My name is Singha. I believe my story can bring hope and spirit to the readers. I am 34 and was born in a middle-class Indian family. I have an elder brother (our age difference is seven years).

From the very beginning, as I started realizing things, it became clear that I was an unwanted child. My grandparents wanted my parents to have another child, and that's why I was born. I realized my elder brother had all my parents' attention – he got everything as a boy, but growing up, I was neglected and not cherished. I wanted to play soccer and other sports, but my parents were so strict toward me that they never allowed me to pursue any sports as a career. My elder brother had the best food and clothes, but I didn't get any of my choices. That's how it was. After my primary schooling, I just couldn't take all the suffering, and when I was 10, I went to an ashram and started living there. I learned yoga and other meditation techniques. My parents had no contact with me. I used to do many hard jobs in my childhood to get food and other things even though I couldn't complete my formal education due to lack of money. My parents and my family were having their own lives during that time. They were never interested in knowing where I was and how I was. I accumulated anger and hate for them, and I was completely detached from my family.

After coming out of the ashram, I made friends who were all addicted to alcohol and weed, and I also started drinking and smoking. Those were the worst days of my life. I was damaging my health and losing sense of my life's purpose. That went on for seven or eight years. I became completely addicted because inside of me, there was a thought I couldn't get rid of: that my parents and my family didn't want me, and I was an unwanted child.

They have abused me. I gathered so much hate and anger for them that I never wanted to see them again.

Suddenly, one day, I met one of my old teachers. He had just returned from The Himalayas to the city and called me to meet him. I didn't want to meet him, and I didn't know what came to my mind, so I decided to go. I was stoned while I was meeting him. He realized this, and he noticed things about me. He invited me to join his ashram. I continually said no for a few days, but after one month, I went to his ashram and started living there. After a few days, I started doing meditation and yoga again, and I stopped drinking altogether. I thought this was going to be my fight from all the traumas and emotions that I have cultivated from my family. After a few years, I released all the trauma.

Now, I have become a kind of Yogi monk. I don't have any reaction. I'm still trying to get rid of my ego anger, and I learned to forgive so that I have no anger for my family and parents now. They are living their lives. I don't meet them, but I don't feel any anger toward them. Now, I am peaceful and happy. I want to tell those who gathered anger for the abusers in their lives it is hard to forgive - I know that, but anger brings nothing. It only burns inside and takes away all of the peace and calmness. We should come out from all the trauma for ourselves. We should gather love and blessings by doing helpful things. I'm sure my story will provide hope and strength for many.
Thank you for the opportunity to share my story.

-Singha

Not sure how it began
But it did
I think I was seven
In the silage pit
We all played there
All of us
Touching
New things
I didn't know what it was
I am one of nine children
It went on and on
The attention was scary
And fascinating
Felt incredible
Like I was special
One of a kind
I ravished the attention
More and more
I didn't know what it was
It continued it continued
He was older
He had girlfriends
I thought he was so cool
At least, that was what I thought
One day, we went for a drive
Yes, he had a car
I think I was 12 or 11
Not sure
We started kissing
Fooling around
Next thing he was on top of me
Yes
Totally on top of me
It got intense
I said no
Repeatedly
It didn't stop

I was freaking out
Totally freaking out
He said it was ok
I said no, no
Then he was inside me
I froze like a board
Crazed
Scared
Terrified
Was it all over
Then he pulled out
And came on my stomach
Scarred for life
Terrified
Frozen
I just lay there for a moment
Violated
Was it my fault
I put myself there
Why
Destroyed
It's taken me years
I'll never be the same.

– Anonymous

He sexually abused all the kids in the family – possibly my brothers, too. I knew it was wrong, so I told my dad about it. He hugged me. My aunt yelled. Later, when I was 14, I saw him and refused to kiss him. I buried this memory all these years. Then, during the last 25 years, I heard from other cousins that they had similar stories.

When I was eight, they served chicken casserole for lunch at my school. I didn't like it, so I didn't eat it. My teacher threatened that if I didn't eat it, I couldn't play. Then she locked me in the classroom and made me eat it.

Another time, the teacher chopped a piece of my hair off, grabbed me by the hair, washed my mouth out with soap, and hit me on the back with a ruler.

-Victoria

1980

There were signs (I ignored them). My friends tried to warn me (they were jealous). He was sorry (every time), and we were happy (weren't we). It's true… *"The cruelest lies of all the lies we tell are the ones we tell ourselves."*

We were high school sweethearts - destined to escape the turbulent upbringings we had both experienced. At 15, I didn't know much, but I did know he was my everything. Even when he drank too much, was overly aggressive, or took other girls out on dates…I found a way to excuse it all. He was always sorry. The following spring, he joined the Marines at 17 and left for Iceland. That fall, he was dishonorably discharged for volatile behavior. I was elated. We fell back in step, and life barreled on. At 17, I was pregnant, and when I told my parents, things were clearly laid out for me. My father told me, "You made your bed; now lie in it." And I did.

1984

We married after high school and had two children. The abuse was always there, like a birthmark or a scar. It was visible - but I did my best to keep it covered. After a while, no one mentioned it. My friends all disappeared, and I was always closely monitored. It didn't get better; it just became "my normal," and our kids saw it all. For me, that was the worst. It's been 40+ years, and that one fact has been hardest for me to transmute. I 100% believed = I did this - but they suffered = there were times I felt defeated enough to tell him I was leaving. I believed he hated our life as much as I did. We were both miserable. These moments would send him into a violent rage, and soon enough, the shoving, emotional/verbal abuse, and punishments morphed into closed fists, threats against my family, and suicidal ideation.

1989

One night just before Christmas, I was fixing dinner and preparing to leave for my waitressing job. The kids were already eating, and as I placed my husband's dinner in front of him, I asked him if he wanted bread. I walked back toward the sink, and he didn't answer, so I turned toward him and was hit by the plate of spaghetti he threw at my head. It wasn't the spaghetti on my face that did it. It was "the looks." His look of absolute hatred and disgust and the looks on the faces of both my babies. Not fear, not confusion. Pure Sadness. They knew this scene; they knew how to respond. They sprung into action.

My then almost 2-year-old son reached for his favorite stuffy and went toward the door. My then almost 6-year-old daughter dragged the chair toward the wall where the telephone hung and attempted to call my mom. I turned to my husband and said, "We are leaving. We are not doing this anymore." He began screaming, throwing things, and repeatedly punching the wall near my face until his knuckles bled. My brother, who had been staying in the basement, heard the commotion and came up the stairs as my husband was tearing the phone away from our daughter and off the wall. He chased my brother back down the stairs and then looked at me and said, "If you're leaving me, it's in a body bag." He headed for the bedroom, where I knew he kept his gun. As he opened the closet, I grabbed both kids and ran. No coats, no shoes. It was cold, and there was a lot of snow, but we managed to get to the woods at the end of our street before he pulled out of the driveway. We hid in the pines as he drove by. My face was bloodied. My clothes were torn, and I was trembling from head to toe, but my children were physically unharmed, and for the moment, we were safe. I had no idea what had happened to my brother or how we would get help, but I saw our truck passing by within minutes and knew he was looking for us. He was driving slowly but didn't see us, so he kept going. Another 2 to 3 minutes and I saw cruiser lights. The officer pulled into my driveway, and I ran as quickly as possible toward the house. He saw us and escorted us to the cruiser. I began telling him through sobs what had happened, and he said he was there because my brother had reported it from a neighbor's house.

My mom pulled up shortly after the officer got us into the cruiser. Although my daughter hadn't been able to speak to her before the phone was destroyed, Mom realized something was wrong and headed to the house immediately. The officer asked my mother to take the children, and I stayed in the cruiser so that we could try to locate my husband. He wanted me to identify the truck if possible.

Mom and the kids headed back to her house, and we headed up the road to look for my husband. By this point, I was starting to come down from the absolute shock I'd been in and felt as if I were going to vomit at any moment. And then I saw the headlights and knew he was coming toward us. I came unglued. I knew he had the gun. I knew he wanted me dead. I came close to passing out. We turned around and got to the house just as my husband climbed the front stairs. The officer drew his weapon and had my husband put his hands up against the door. He cuffed and put him in the cruiser, and I returned to the house. He was charged with domestic violence, but because he had left the loaded 357 Magnum on the seat in the truck, they chose not to charge him with attempted murder. Had he either still been in the truck or had the gun on him when he headed for the house, the entire event would have ended differently.

I was granted a restraining order, and my husband moved in with my mother. He had no family, and dysfunction was so normal in my life that it just seemed logical at the time. I genuinely don't know how! After a couple of days, he started talking about suicide and was admitted to a mental health facility. He was there for a month and diagnosed bipolar. The restraining order lapsed, and we fell right back into the same routine for another five years. The first 3 to 4 months were mild, but it wasn't long before he began acting just as abusive, and now he had a new routine. When I talked back or disagreed with him, or God forbid, protected the kids from his outbursts, he'd take me by my hair, squeeze the back of my neck, and lead me to our bedroom, where he'd make me look out the window. There, he'd tell me the story of how he was going to kill me for being such a C@&t. He was going to make me suffer like I made him suffer every day, and he was going to enjoy every minute of it. The plan was to tie me to a chair and make me watch as, one by one, he doused our children in gasoline and lit them on fire. Once they were both dead, he'd come to get me. Again, with the gasoline, but he'd start at the other end of the house because he wanted my death to be slow so I'd "never forget how long pain lasts." He was very calm when reciting his plan. He was so sure of himself, and I truly believed him. I knew he'd do it, and so I stayed. Oh, and at this point, he let me know he was no longer sorry. I did this. I made him this way, and I'd get what I had coming.

1994

I began selling real estate in 1994, and I believe having new people around me somehow empowered me. I started hiding money (a few dollars here or there) for the day we could escape, and my very wise Real Estate Broker/boss intuitively knew things were bad. She would share stories with me of her abusive ex-husband, and somehow, that gave me strength. She was always so happy, perky, and confident. All the things I knew I'd never be, but I felt for the first time hopeful. It was only a little bit of hope, but still so much more than I'd ever felt.

At home, things were no better. He and I no longer really talked. We just exchanged verbal jabs and lived under the same roof. I was becoming like him. I could feel it, and I hated it. He drank every day, was verbally cruel to the kids, and always made sure I never forgot he had a plan. I drank, too; a six-pack or more a night was what it took to get me through.

1996
And then it happened—the breaking point. One gloriously random Sunday morning, I was serving breakfast to my children. They loved pancakes and bacon, and it was always a Sunday treat. I put two pancakes on my daughter's plate, and as I walked back to the stove, I heard him say, "Eat all that, and you'll be a fat pig just like her." I turned around and whipped the spatula at his head. I'd snapped - I lost it. I was going to be responsible for the deaths of my beautiful children and also myself. But at that moment, I knew just one thing: death was better than this.

He was shocked. The kids were shocked. Hell, I was stunned. I had never before (and never since) thrown an object at another person in anger. But here's the part we didn't see coming. *He did nothing.* Not a damn thing. And then he begged, and pleaded, and promised he'd change. Over the next few weeks, he went to counseling, where he lied through his teeth; it failed. He stalked me, so I got restraining orders, and he continuously broke them. He called relentlessly to harass me, so I changed my number repeatedly. He refused to pay support or even see his kids, and he spiraled. Wow, he spiraled. He almost died more than once. But this time was different. I no longer feared him. It had all been bravado, and he had never followed through. We were finally free. The truth is, we struggled, the kids and I. It was often quite challenging, but it was still better. We went to counseling, and in some areas, we succeeded, while in other areas, we failed, but we never surrendered. We've all walked away with some of the trauma and harrowing memories, but the glorious part is that *We Walked Away*. We're still picking up pieces. Finding the lessons and letting go. We're survivors, and we're going to be OK -

-LM

Attachment patterns

I grew up with three older brothers. Some would say, "Oh, you must be so spoiled." Yes. In some ways, I was spoiled. My eldest brother made sure he brought me out to museums to get me out of the house. There was a lot of fighting at home between my parents. I felt protected by him and loved. Safe.

My middle brother would often take me to his softball games. I was in charge of holding all the keys, sunglasses, jackets, etc. I felt important.

The youngest of my brothers hated me from day one (actually, before day one). And, ironically, I understood why. My little empath self always got what was happening around me - probably more than my family members.

I often got the message that I was the youngest, so I didn't "know" anything. I was the only girl, so I didn't "know" anything. Unfortunately, I internalized these messages for many years, and despite being highly capable, even from a young age, I felt I *didn't* know much. Thankfully, in my 58th year, I can say differently. I have done so much and been through so much! I have worked hard to heal.

I joined The Navy straight out of high school - skipped prom, and went to boot camp. I met my Dad at The Carlyle Hotel for lunch that day to celebrate. I went to an elite high school even though math and science were not my thing. I got through four challenging years at a super academic college, which, in retrospect, was probably not for me. I was date raped in college by a black student who purposely violated and impregnated white women. I got pregnant and terminated the pregnancy. That was one of the hardest years of my life. I was 17.

My brother seemed to delight in being mean to me. I felt scared being with him alone. I remember one night when my parents went out, and he and I were left alone with the sitter. I was scared. I think I even said, please don't leave me with him. He filled the bathtub and threw me in the bath, fully dressed. I guess you could call it a kind of "psychological torture" that I felt in his presence. I remember one summer in Florida, he put me up on the pool table. It was some kind of punishment, I guess. I was so angry and scared that I did not realize that I could have easily gotten down by myself - it was only a few feet down. That is the power of our minds, both for positive and negative reasons.

As the years went by, I distanced myself from him, but not after many years of trying to be his friend and get him to like me and spend time with me.

In my twenties, after I had met my future husband, we attended my brother's wedding. He introduced me as his half-sister. I was devastated. I went to the bathroom and cried.

This trend of "otherness" unfortunately continued. My second oldest brother was sadly made to do many things when we were growing up that would cause him to resent me. That was not my doing, but my mother's, as she was overwhelmed and did not have much support or help. I can remember during the "anthrax" period - post 9/11, he would send me these hateful letters, blaming me for having to take care of me as a child, having to bring me to school, etc. Thankfully, I was far along enough in my healing journey to be able to deflect his anger to the appropriate source. My therapist at the time offered to hold his letters for me. We would later call them the "anthrax letters." I finally wrote him a letter and suggested that he speak with our mother about what he was angry about and what he resented. There were many times in my life that I was not able to do this and internalized whatever crap was being flung at me.

Part of the difficult dynamic began way before I was conceived. My mother had three children: two from her first marriage and one from her most recent marriage. When she met my father and decided to have me, my relationship with my brothers was rigged from the start. Later in my life, I would come to know that most of them never really considered me their full-blown sister but their "half-sister" at best.

When I look at my recent relationships, my nearly 30-year marriage, and other causal/more committed/serious relationships I have been a part of, I realize it all goes back to my attachment patterns. My parents both loved me very much. I know this, and I know I am much better off than others who didn't receive that love. However, given their respective trauma, they were often inconsistent in their ability to be present for me emotionally.

My mother had four children and worked full-time. Unfortunately, she did not have partners who were supportive and helpful. They tried but were limited for different reasons.

My father had multiple traumas before the age of 25. He had lost his mother very young - under age 3. His father, not knowing or perhaps not caring, put the five children in an orphanage. I found out later that my paternal grandfather was an alcoholic, probably with his own innate trauma. My father fought in Korea, and like many veterans, he was in his early 20s. He saw his best friend killed in front of him, powerless to do anything to help. A piece of shrapnel injured him, and he would live with a disability his entire life that made walking difficult and painful. My father told the story that the Army medics wanted to amputate his leg. He refused, and when he did, he was told he would be sent back to the front lines. So he left. Deserted. In wartime, this is punishable by death. He went to Japan and met one of the great loves of his life, Michiko. But that is for another story…

Getting back to attachment patterns, because of my father's alcoholism and trauma and because of my mother's overwhelm and anger, I never really knew which parent I was getting. Would it be the nurturing, loving, sensitive, and affectionate father? The angry mother who scared me? The father who came home from work, had a few martinis, and slept until dinner? The mother who provided for us and helped me to become my determined and feisty self?

I have worked on myself for many years….almost 40. I am 57. It is the greatest gift you can give yourself, your kids, and your great-grandchildren whom you will never meet. So, I leave you with this query: Who am I?

– JT

Dear Me -

It's time we had a difficult conversation, one that touches upon the deep wounds you've been carrying for far too long. Over the span of 20 years, you've endured unspeakable pain at the hands of multiple men, each inflicting their own brand of cruelty upon you. From the horror of one allowing a dog to attack you to the betrayal of another stealing your hard-earned money and the agony of one breaking your arm so severely that you needed a metal plate, the trauma you've endured is unimaginable.

It's heartbreaking to acknowledge the toll these experiences have taken on your mental and emotional well-being. The sense of worthlessness and despair that has plagued you, driving you back into the arms of those who have hurt you time and time again, is a burden no one should have to bear. It's no wonder that amidst this sea of pain, you found solace in substances, leading to a battle with heroin addiction and countless other addictions as a means of coping with the overwhelming weight of your trauma.

But I want you to know that you are not defined by the suffering you've endured. You are resilient, courageous, and deserving of love and healing. It's okay to reach out for help, to lean on the support of those who care about you, and to seek professional guidance as you navigate the path toward recovery. You have the strength within you to break free from the cycle of abuse and addiction, reclaim your sense of self-worth, and rebuild your life on your own terms.

Please remember that you are worthy of love, happiness, and healing. You are not alone in this journey, and there are people who will stand by you, offering their unwavering support and encouragement every step of the way. You have survived the unimaginable, and now it's time to reclaim your power and rewrite your story.

With love and compassion,

-Lynsey Brown

The truth is the hardest part for me overcoming the religious cult was finally having the strength to leave it, stay out of it, rebuild my life on my terms, and speak out about my experiences of the religious trauma I experienced on that path.

When you are in a religious cult, you do not realize it while it is happening, but they brainwash you. They somehow influence everything you think or do. Whether it be the leader telling you what you can or cannot do or just leading everyone down a road by teaching them a belief that is the ultimate belief on how things should be done. Almost everything you do is somehow connected to the cult. The food you eat, the music you listen to, how you use your finances, what you wear, your hairstyles, make-up selections, and so forth. However, because the brainwashing happens so slowly, you do not realize it is there. You think what you do is normal and the only way to do things. I think I knew I was brainwashed, even though I was forced to be in the cult by my parents and tried hard to see through the false teaching as it came to me. I was still caught in the in-between of trying not to believe the teachings and think for myself but practicing everything they taught perfectly so I would not get in trouble or punished. So, the beliefs seeped in, and I guess they took hold without me recognizing it. Well, until I left, I recognized it a lot.

While I was in the cult, I saw a lot of abuse by the leaders at play—some physical, but primarily mental, spiritual, and emotional. A lot of hypocrisy was at play. The whole foundation was set up as a patriarchal gateway for men to be over women. What the man said – it went for everyone. You were not allowed to debate it or question it. He was the authority, and women were shamed. If something terrible happened to them, they stepped out of the "umbrella" of authority or protection of the man, causing the bad thing to happen. If a man sexually abused you, it was never the man's fault. Instead, the religious leaders would point to the woman and say she was being seductive with her dress or actions. There was never true justice for the men, just the women. And there was always a double standard.

You learned to tell them what they wanted to hear so you wouldn't get hurt. That was hard for me because I couldn't stand to see things happening that were wrong. I could not say anything—the few times I chose to use my voice, I was discredited, made to believe I was crazy, told not to tell others (including my parents), and even locked up in a room with zero food or water for three days. I watched my childhood belongings be burned in front of me, and anything I had that was not approved was stripped from me and thrown away. They knew how to break you until you lost your "rational" thinking enough to bend to their thinking.

Deciding to leave for me was not a question of **IF** it would happen, but instead, **WHEN** it would happen. I knew I would be an outcast, and I knew my parents would disown me. I had to ensure I was ready to face whatever was before me on the other side. Leaving for me was not going to be accessible in itself because the cult had a way of mentally making you second guess yourself and stripping you of any customary rights you might have. For example, my parents chose my clothes, how I wore my hair, the music I listened to, the friends I could talk to, and even the money I earned. It was all in their control. I was never allowed to think for myself or find my own way. I had no friends. I had no job. I had no vehicle. It is how they work. To seclude you so that you cannot leave. I did not have a vehicle, a regular job, or was allowed to go to college (they were against women getting higher level education). You never have enough space to begin thinking about who you are and what you want with your life—no space to develop your belief system or the allowance to do so.

The Universe divinely worked for me when I started to think about leaving. Since I was so limited in my freedom, one of the few things that my parents allowed with zero issues was religious materials. So, I told my mom I wanted to do a Bible study on my own of a lady who, at the time, was hugely popular for her material. The particular study was about breaking free of legalism and replacing it with a faith that had grace. It's funny how I can now see holes in even her teaching, but at that time, it was her teaching that led me to be strong enough to leave the cult. I remember using her material to invalidate what was being told to me from the religious cult. Slowly, I started to untie the beliefs that left me bound to stay in the cult for fear of leaving. The fact I could even do that in the state of deep depression I was in at the time, to me now, seems incomprehensible.

It was six months past my eighteenth birthday, and I had, in most ways, just bought my time until I was mentally ready to leave, but no one can ever be fully prepared for leaving a life behind that is ingrained in you. I was babysitting for a couple (he was an influential doctor in my local town) to attend a hospital Christmas party. I knew they would be late, and the kids would fall asleep. My parents dropped me off at their house, and as always, I was supposed to call them when I was ready to leave so they could get me. Before I left to babysit that night, I looked around my room and knew I was not returning to the prison it represented for me. I packed a change of clothes, my favorite books, my wallet, and a few pictures. It was all I could pack in my backpack without looking suspicious. Despite my parents saying I was a problem child, I honestly lived my life to their every whim and never snuck out, dated behind their backs, ran away from home, did drugs, or anything even remotely out of line in their book of rules. That night, I called an acquaintance I knew had left her parents' home because she would understand my predicament, and I asked her to help me. She was in college, and she came to pick me up. The next few weeks were blurry. I mainly shuffled from house to house until I settled in with my dad's brother to save the family some "face." It was from this point that I started to let myself explore life, and yes, I made a hell of a lot of mistakes.

Even during the early weeks of my leaving home, I began to realize how deep the cult was ingrained in me. I remember standing in a department store trying to buy clothes so I had something to wear (my parents refused to give me my stuff), and I was frozen. Was I supposed to pick out what I wanted and buy it? Anything I wanted? I didn't need approval or to ask someone else or think about "if" I could wear it based on a set of rules. It was hard for me to grasp that concept, and it took several years to figure out what I liked about clothes and what I felt like. Another time, my uncle's vehicle had a blowout while we were on our way somewhere, I immediately thought it was my fault they had the blowout because I was out of my "umbrella of authority." At one point, my parents were so upset about me leaving home that they told me on the phone they were praying I got cancer to bring me back to God (they might have said that slightly differently, but that was the jest of what they meant). I got off the phone and was devastated. Their cult meant more than their daughter. It meant decades later, I refused to tell my parents of my cancer diagnosis because of that statement they had made so many years earlier. I wrestled with issues of thinking I deserved it. It was small things like this that happened daily, and looking back, I am in awe of how I was brainwashed.

I wish I could say that I found myself and things were better, but I had no idea who I was or how even to find myself. It was a slow process of finding myself that would take many decades to uncover. Therapy was helpful a lot in the first five years of leaving the cult. It helped me to not feel guilty about everything that happened in life. It helped me to realize I had trauma and CPTSD. It helped me to realize what emotional blackmail was and selfish control. If I could give one piece of advice for those leaving religious trauma, it is to get professional help from someone who specializes in that particular field. For the first few sessions, I would say "religious organization," and my therapist would keep saying "cult." It was hard for me to accept it was a cult, and when I did accept it and start to use the term - it made so much more sense. Therapy in those early years gave me a lot of my life back. It was one of the best decisions I ever made. My therapist was amazing, and to this day, I sing her praises anytime someone asks me about my recovery. Whenever I felt guilty about an everyday decision, she would point me back to "Is your decision hurting someone intentionally?" When I said no, she would say, then let it go – it is misplaced guilt. I learned to sift through so many guilty emotions that were just not actual guilt.

Taking control of my life back was a process that eventually involved me talking publicly about how the cult had affected my life. I thought I was ready for that and that it would bring justice to them, but instead, it created many problems for me. My parents issued statements against me to the press, and the cult started following me and threatening me. I ended up with charges that eventually were expunged thanks to a fantastic probation officer who saw how I had been framed to be silenced. I started having a lot of nightmares about the cult, and they succeeded; I shut up. To this day, I do not talk about my experience, and until this letter, I have kept quiet about most of everything that happened to me in those years. Even now, I will not talk in detail about it because what happened does not matter nearly as much as how it affected me my entire life afterward.

I went through stages where I was sure I was an atheist because I was trying to make sense of religion. Then, I went through phases where I was devoutly religious. I was mixed up, and it took a long time to iron out what I believed and not what someone wanted me to believe. I eventually repaired my relationship with my parents, but it is still strained when it comes to religion. They have never admitted that they were wrong or that it is a cult. Instead, they moved from that cult to other cult-like belief systems. My therapist told me in my early years of therapy that people who are drawn to cults will always be drawn to them because they crave someone to tell them what to believe. They do not know what they genuinely believe for themselves. I have found that to be true. Most of my life in the cult is blacked out in my memories now. A lot of those years have giant black holes. I have tried hard to make sure I did not pass along religious trauma to my children, which mainly resulted in being open with them so that they could form their own opinions of religion or what they believed without any judgment or influence from me. I trust them to be their person.

Do I still have days where it gets in my head? Yes.

Do I have days when I am triggered and cry? Yes.

Do I still catch myself thinking ingrained beliefs? Sometimes.

However, I have gone on to lead a happy and fulfilled life. I have slowly accepted myself and am working hard to take my worthiness in life. Worthiness has been a HUGE issue for me to overcome. Women were lesser than creatures, and my very existence was bigger than it should have been as a child. I remember always wanting to be famous or speak to large crowds and would pretend to do so in the mirror on my dresser. That "prideful" action caused my mirror to be removed and never returned to me until I left home and got my own mirror. Anytime I did something well or said something about what I had done, I was cut down and immediately told I would fail for being proud. It caused me to shut down, and even now, I do not trust myself or my work to be good enough. I have worked hard the past couple of years, specifically to work on seeing my value and owning it. I was trusting myself enough to put my work into the world. The worthiness issues have even caused me to entangle myself in relationships that were not only unhealthy but the product of domestic violence.

Religious trauma is complex, and it takes a long time to recover from. A lifetime, actually. So be kind to yourself and keep pressing on. You have got this, and you are breaking generational trauma; that is **NEVER** easy. You can find so much of your peace and beliefs hidden inside you the more you allow yourself the ability to unlock who you indeed are. Keep your chin up, and when you need support, get it.

I am thankful for all my therapists, supportive partners, spiritual leaders, and even for my medication, who all helped me find a better version of myself.

When healing from religious trauma – it takes a village.

May you find healing within,

-Blair Hayse

Messages Of Hope

We collected some messages from those who have struggled with abuse, bullying & cults on:

"What help/advice can you offer someone who is going through a similar situation?"

Here were their unedited answers to messages of hope they wanted to share with you:

"Face it, go within. The hero is inside. It is YOU bathed in total Love."

"Find safety first. Then seek help. It's difficult to weed through thoughts that are disguised at best."

"Take a deep breath. Now take another one. Continue to take deep breaths. Sometimes that's all you can do, just breathe. There is no perfect formula for healing. No real guidebook on how to process and move on. You don't have to be completely okay again. You choose your timeline. You make the decisions. You, no one else. You process, you adjust, you breath on your own terms. Eventually, hopefully, one day, you'll be able to breath without fear. "Your healing cannot depend on the other person admitting the damage that they have caused you. Because more often than not, they won't admit it. It is entirely on you to heal what they broke in you." ~Kayil York"

"Know your worth we are all worthy I thought I wasn't because I wasn't smart at school and that compounded in me over years."

"Stay in the moment."

"It's important to remove yourself from toxic environments and toxic relationships. What they are saying to you is more a reflection of themselves. Everyone has a purpose and a reason that they are here. We all have value. My favourite quote: Be who you are and say what you feel. Those that mind, don't matter and those that matter don't mind. Dr. Seuss"

"Just keep pushing through."

Appendix on Support Resources

Includes Links, Numbers, & Resources For Abuse, Bullying, & Cults

Bullying:

www.stopbullying.gov

https://www.crisistextline.org/topics/bullying/#what-is-bullying-1

www.stompoutbullying.org

Cyberbullying:

https://www.cybersmile.org/advice-help/category/who-to-call

Spiritual Abuse:

https://www.thehotline.org/resources/what-is-spiritual-abuse/

United States Resources:

National Sexual Assault Hotline: 800 656 HOPE

or www.rainn.org

(Rape, abuse, and incest national hotline)

National Domestic Violence Hotline: 800 787 7233

or www.thehotline.org

Planned Parenthood Hotline: 800 230 7526

or *www.plannedparenthood.org*

Find support.

Appendix on Suicide Resources

**Includes Resources for
Suicide Help & Assessment**

List of Suicide Help & Hotlines[1]:
(United States and Worldwide)

United States:
Emergency: 911
Suicide Hotline: 988

Algeria:
Emergency: 34342 and 43
Suicide Hotline: 0021 3983 2000 58

Angola:
Emergency: 113

Argentina:
Emergency: 911
Suicide Hotline: 135

Armenia:
Emergency: 911 and 112
Suicide Hotline: (2) 538194

---

[1] List of Helplines and Hotline Numbers Retrieved from
blog.opencounseling.com

Australia:
Emergency: 000
Suicide Hotline: 131114

Austria:
Emergency: 112
Telefonseelsorge 24/7 142
Rat auf Draht 24/7 147 (Youth)

Bahamas:
Emergency: 911
Suicide Hotline: (2) 322-2763

Bahrain:
Emergency: 999

Bangladesh:
Emergency: 999

Barbados:
Emergency: 911
Suicide Hotline Samaritan Barbados: (246) 4299999

Belgium:
Emergency: 112
Suicide Hotline Stichting Zelfmoordlijn: 1813

Bolivia:
Emergency: 911
Suicide Hotline: 3911270

Bosnia & Herzegovina:
Suicide Hotline: 080 05 03 05

Botswana:
Emergency: 911
Suicide Hotline: +2673911270

Brazil:
Emergency: 188

Bulgaria:
Emergency: 112
Suicide Hotline: 0035 9249 17 223

Burundi:
Emergency: 117

Burkina Faso:
Emergency: 17

Canada:
Emergency: 911
Suicide Hotline: 1 (822) 456 4566

Chad:
Emergency: 2251-1237

China:
Emergency: 110
Suicide Hotline: 800-810-1117

Columbia:
24/7 Helpline in Barranquilla: 1(00 57 5) 372 27 27
24/7 Hotline Bogota: (57-1 323 24 25

Congo:
Emergency: 117

Costa Rica:
Emergency: 911
Suicide Hotline: 506-253-5439

Croatia:
Emergency: 112

Cyprus:
Emergency: 112
Suicide Hotline: 8000 7773

Czech Republic:
Emergency: 112

Denmark:
Emergency: 112
Suicide Hotline: 4570201201

Dominican Republic:
Emergency: 911
Suicide Hotline: (809) 562-3500

Ecuador:
Emergency: 911

Egypt:
Emergency: 122
Suicide Hotline: 131114

El Salvador:
Emergency: 911
Suicide Hotline: 126

Equatorial Guinea:
Emergency: 114

Estonia:
Emergency: 112
Suicide Hotline: 3726558088
In Russian: 3726555688

Ethiopia:
Emergency: 911

Finland:
Emergency: 112
Suicide Hotline: 010 195 202

France:
Emergency: 112
Suicide Hotline: 0145394000

Germany:
Emergency: 112
Suicide Hotline: 0800 111 0 111

Ghana:
Emergency: 999
Suicide Hotline: 2332 444 71279

Greece:
Emergency: 1018

Guatemala:
Emergency: 110
Suicide Hotline: 5392-5953

Guinea:
Emergency: 117

Guinea Bissau:
Emergency: 117

Guyana:
Emergency: 999
Suicide Hotline: 223-0001

Holland:
Suicide Hotline: 09000767

Hong Kong:
Emergency: 999
Suicide Hotline: 852 2382 0000

Hungary:
Emergency: 112
Suicide Hotline: 116123

India:
Emergency: 112
Suicide Hotline: 8888817666

Indonesia:
Emergency: 112
Suicide Hotline: 1-800-273-8255

Iran:
Emergency: 110
Suicide Hotline: 1480

Ireland:
Emergency: 116123
Suicide Hotline: +4408457909090

Israel:
Emergency: 100
Suicide Hotline: 1201

Italy:
Emergency: 112
Suicide Hotline: 800860022

Jamaica:
Suicide Hotline: 1-888-429-KARE (5273)

Japan:
Emergency: 110
Suicide Hotline: 810352869090

Jordan:
Emergency: 911
Suicide Hotline: 110

Kenya:
Emergency: 999
Suicide Hotline: 722178177

Kuwait:
Emergency: 112
Suicide Hotline: 94069304

Latvia:
Emergency: 113
Suicide Hotline: 371 67222922

Lebanon:
Suicide Hotline: 1564

Liberia:
Emergency: 911
Suicide Hotline: 6534308

Luxembourg:
Emergency: 112
Suicide Hotline: 352 45 45 45

Madagascar:
Emergency: 117

Malaysia:
Emergency: 999
Suicide Hotline: (06) 2842500

Mali:
Emergency: 8000-1115

Malta:
Suicide Hotline: 179

Mauritius:
Emergency: 112
Suicide Hotline: +230 800 93 93

Mexico:
Emergency: 911
Suicide Hotline: 5255102550

Netherlands:
Emergency: 112
Suicide Hotline: 900 0113

New Zealand:
Emergency: 111
Suicide Hotline: 1737

Niger:
Emergency: 112

Nigeria:
Suicide Hotline: 234 8092106493

Norway:
Emergency: 112
Suicide Hotline: +4781533300

Pakistan:
Emergency: 115

Peru:
Emergency: 911
Suicide Hotline: 381-3695

Philippines:
Emergency: 911
Suicide Hotline: 028969191

Poland:
Emergency: 112
Suicide Hotline: 5270000

Portugal:
Emergency: 112
Suicide Hotline: 21 854 07 40
And 8 96 898 21 50

Qatar:
Emergency: 999

Romania:
Emergency: 112
Suicide Hotline: 0800 801200

Russia:
Emergency: 112
Suicide Hotline: 0078202577577

Saint Vincent and the Grenadines:
Suicide Hotline: 9784 456 1044

São Tomé and Príncipe:
Suicide Hotline: (239) 222-12-22 ext. 123

Saudi Arabia:
Emergency: 112

Serbia:
Suicide Hotline: (+381) 21-6623-393

Senegal:
Emergency: 17

Singapore:
Emergency: 999
Suicide Hotline: 1 800 2214444

Spain:
Emergency: 112
Suicide Hotline: 914590050

South Africa:
Emergency: 10111
Suicide Hotline: 0514445691

South Korea:
Emergency: 112
Suicide Hotline: (02) 7158600

Sri Lanka:
Suicide Hotline: 011 057 2222662

Sudan:
Suicide Hotline: (249) 11-555-253

Sweden:
Emergency: 112
Suicide Hotline: 46317112400

Switzerland:
Emergency: 112
Suicide Hotline: 143

Tanzania:
Emergency: 112

Thailand:
Suicide Hotline: (02) 713-6793

Tonga:
Suicide Hotline: 23000

Trinidad and Tobago:
Suicide Hotline: (868) 645 2800

Tunisia:
Emergency: 197

Turkey:
Emergency: 112

Uganda:
Emergency: 112
Suicide Hotline: 0800 21 21 21

United Arab Emirates:
Suicide Hotline: 800 46342

United Kingdom:
Emergency: 112
Suicide Hotline: 0800 689 5652

United States:
Emergency: 911
Suicide Hotline: 988

Zambia:
Emergency: 999
Suicide Hotline: +260960264040

Zimbabwe:
Emergency: 999
Suicide Hotline: 080 12 333 333

Conduct a Suicide Inquiry[2]

a. Ideation

Frequency, Intensity and Duration

- Have you had thoughts of hurting yourself or others?
- Have you thought about ending your life?

Now, in the Past, and at its Worst

- During the last 48 hours, past month, and worst ever: How much? How intense? Lasting for how long?

b. Plan

Timing, Location, Lethality, Availability/Means

- When you think about killing yourself or ending your life, what do you imagine?
- When? Where? How would you do it? In what way?

---

[2] Retrieved from Minnesota Department of Health at: https://www.health.state.mn.us/people/syringe/suicide.pdf

Preparatory Acts

- What steps have you taken to prepare to kill yourself, if any?

c. Behavior

Past attempts, aborted attempts, rehearsals

- Have you ever thought about or tried to kill yourself in the past?
- Have you ever taken any actions to rehearse or practice ending your life (e.g., tying noose, loading gun, measuring substance)?

Non-suicidal self-injurious behavior

- Are you having paranoid thoughts? Hallucinations?
- Have you done anything to hurt yourself (e.g., cutting, burning or mutilation)?

d. Intent

Extent to which they expect to carry out the plan and believe the plan to be lethal versus harmful.

- What do you think will happen?
- What things put you at risk of ending your life or

killing yourself (reasons to die)?
- What things prevent you from killing yourself and keep you safe (reasons to live)?

Explore ambivalence between reasons to die and reasons to live. Pay attention to how they describe the outcome.

- "I'm dead, it's over." indicates a higher risk of suicide death.
- "I think I'd end up in the hospital." indicates a moderate risk of suicide death.
- "I don't want to die; I want my suffering to end." indicates a lower risk of suicide death.

e. **Notes**

- When working with **youth**, collect information from a parent, guardian or service provider on the youth's suicidal thoughts, plans, behaviors, and changes in mood, behavior or disposition.
- If the person has thoughts or plans to **harm someone else**, conduct a homicide inquiry using the same questions (replace "hurt or kill yourself" with "hurt or kill someone else").

Determine Risk Level[3]

The risk level is determined with the previous three steps:

1. Risk Factors
2. Protective Factors
3. Suicide Inquiry

Death by Suicide Risk Level

Risk Level	Risk Factors	Protective Factors	Suicide Inquiry	Intervention*
High	Multiple risk factors	Protective factors are not present or not relevant at this time	Potentially lethal suicide attempt or persistent ideation with strong intent or suicide rehearsal	Hospital admission generally indicated, suicide precautions (e.g., observation, means reduction)
Moderate	Multiple risk factors	Few protective factors	Suicidal ideation with a plan, but not intent or behavior	Hospital admission may be necessary, develop crisis plan and suicide precautions, give emergency/crisis numbers

---

[3] Retrieved from Minnesota Department of Health at: https://www.health.state.mn.us/people/syringe/suicide.pdf

Low	Few and/or modifiable risk factors	Strong protective factors	Thoughts of death with no plan, intent or behavior	Outpatient referral, symptom reduction, give emergency/crisis numbers

Take every suicide attempt seriously!
People often think a person is not really suicidal.
It's better to be safe, even if they will be angry with you for taking action to keep them alive.

About the Author

Jen Taylor, LCSW
#1 International Bestselling Author

Jen Taylor, LCSW is a New York-based spiritual psychotherapist with 23+ years of experience. Jen specializes in womens' empowerment, domestic violence, teens, and LGBTQIA+ individuals. Jen incorporates spirituality and astrology into her sessions to create a truly unique blend of guidance.

Jen was born and raised in New York City and lived there from preschool through high school. Instead of attending her prom, Jen went to boot camp for the Navy and received accreditation as a U.S. Naval photographer. Jen then received her Bachelor's in Arts from Haverford College in Pennsylvania and studied abroad in Florence, Italy. She spent her early 20s in the advertising office of Italian *Vogue* and went on to attend social work school at Fordham University's Graduate school of social services. In 1999, Jen received her Master's in social work while pregnant with her first child, Giancarlo. Jen worked in various outpatient mental health clinics in New York City, and in 2007 had her second child, Elisabetta.

Jen Taylor, LCSW is the editor for Girl on Fire Magazine's "Wine Down with Jen," where she uses her 20+ years of experience as a New York-based spiritual psychotherapist to bring you cozy couch conversations you would have with your best friend over a glass of wine after work.

When not writing for the magazine or seeing clients, Jen enjoys traveling, photography, spending time with her kids, and a good cup of coffee.

Jen is a multiple #1 International bestselling author in a collaboration series and currently working on releasing the rest of this series as her very first solo books over the next year.

To connect with Jen, she can be reached at:

Jentaylorfani@gmail.com